the seeds that grew to be a hundred

Matthew 13:1-17 FOR CHILDREN

Written by Victor Mann   Illustrated by Don Kueker

Concordia
Publishing House
St. Louis

ARCH Books

COPYRIGHT © 1975 CONCORDIA PUBLISHING HOUSE,
ST. LOUIS, MISSOURI

MANUFACTURED IN THE UNITED STATES OF AMERICA

ISBN 0-570-06091-5

Hundreds of people pressed close to Jesus
While He sat by the lake one day.
They had gathered around from every town
To hear what He would say.

They crowded so close He could hardly move.
"A boat is what I need."
So He sat in a boat and told them a tale
Of a farmer planting seed.

A farmer was scattering seeds in his field.
They flew with a whispering sound.
All of them wanted to grow to be healthy.
But some fell on hard, packed ground.

Landing! Bouncing! Rolling! They stopped.
What a terrible place to fall!
At the edge of a path where everyone walked,
How could they ever grow tall?

"Let us in! Let us in! Please let us in!"
The seeds began to cry.
"Our food and water is underground.
If we stay up here we'll die."

People walked by and trampled the seeds,
Crushed them under their feet.
The seeds called loudly, "Help us, please!"
While the birds settled down to eat.

But the hard, packed ground refused to hear,
And the people walked merrily on.
Trampled by feet and eaten by birds,
Soon every seed was gone.

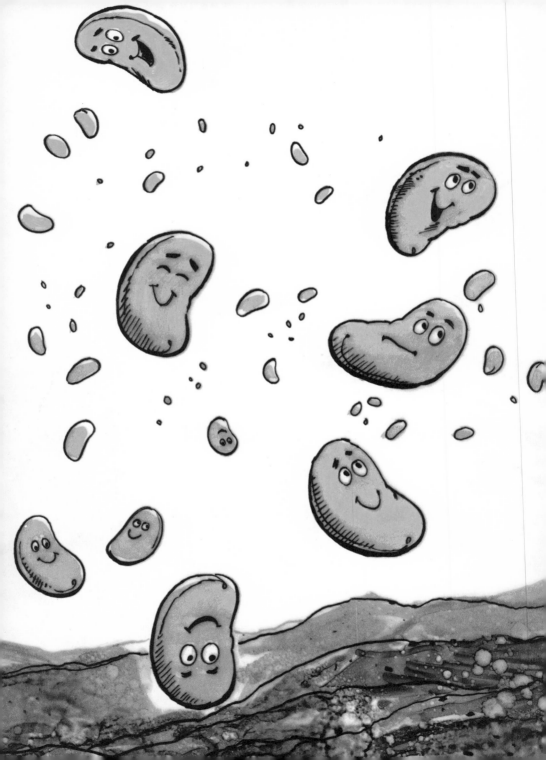

The morning air was speckled with seeds
That flew with a whispering sound.
They wanted to grow to be healthy plants.
But they fell on rocky ground.

It was warm in the soft, thin layer of earth
That covered the cold, hard rock.
And the seeds felt safe because they fell
Where people didn't walk.

Soon tiny pinpoints of green pushed up.
Leaves spread to catch the light.
The roots underground ran out to get food.
Some went left, some down, and some right.

But they ran into rock below shallow earth.
"Move aside. We need to find water."
They wiggled and pushed to get by the rocks.
The ground became dry, the sun hotter.

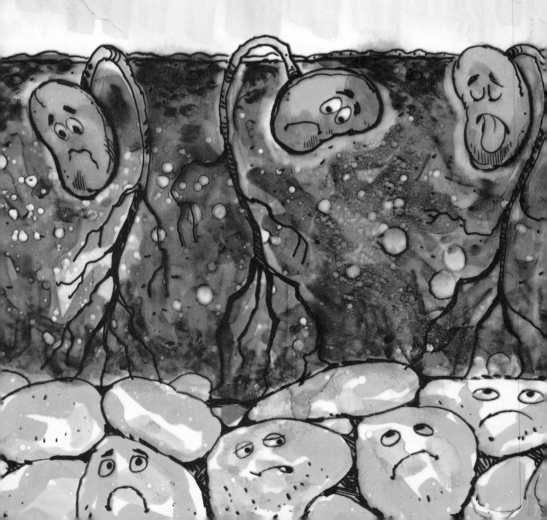

But the rocks didn't care about the plants.
"Remember! We were here first."
Without enough water the plants became weak.
Their heads bowed. They died of thirst.

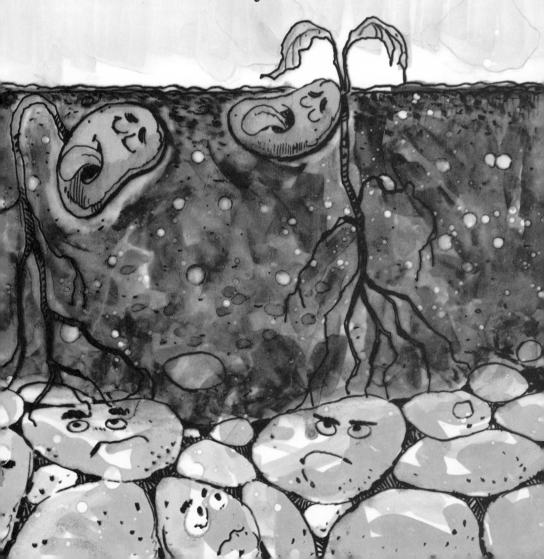

The farmer walked in every direction.
The air was filled with seeds.
They wanted to grow to be healthy and strong.
But the ground was filled with weeds.

Good seeds and weeds grew up side by side.
The weeds and thorns grew fast.
At first they shared food, water, and sun.
But their friendship didn't last.

The weeds grew tall, took over the land.
The thorns grew to be much stronger.
They crowded the plants and blocked the sun.
The plants could take it no longer.

"Move over! Don't crowd! Give us light!
We need more room to grow."
"Harumph! Too bad," said the wicked thorns.
"We're bigger than you are, you know.

"Fight if you like, but we will win."
The laughing thorns sneered with pride.
Fight they did, but the thorns were strong.
The plants grew weak, choked, and died.

The farmer walked on, scattering seeds.
They grew as well as they could.
And some of them did grow tall and strong,
For some of the ground was good.

Asleep in the warm, wet earth they waited
Until it was time to start growing.
Soon out of the earth and into the sunlight
Tiny green sprouts began showing.

Slowly they stretched toward the sky,
Sent deep roots that never got tired
Of gathering food to make the plant grow.
The earth gave them all they desired.

Soon at the top of thin, straight bodies,
Tall, golden heads formed and grew.
Each of those heads had a hundred seeds.
One had a hundred and two.

"We don't understand why you told that story,"
The disciples said when He was done.
"It's our job to preach about God, not farming.
Your story must just be for fun."

"God's Word is like the seeds," said Jesus.
"It goes everywhere to be heard.
But it grows in people, not in the ground,
If their ears will just hear His Word.

"Wherever it grows it causes people to love
Because God loves us all so much.
We learn to love people all over the world,
Most of them too far to touch.

"Now, some people listen, but others don't.
So the meaning of the story is clear.
Don't be like ground where seeds can't grow.
Open your ears and hear."